Rue Traversière

THE
SEAGULL
LIBRARY OF
FRENCH
LITERATURE

Rue Traversière

YVES BONNEFOY

CENTENARY EDITION

Translated by
BEVERLEY BIE BRAHIC

LONDON NEW YORK CALCUTTA

PAP TAGORE

www.bibliofrance.in

The work is published with the support of the
Publication Assistance Programmes of the Institut français

Seagull Books, 2023

First published in French as *Rue Traversière* by Yves Bonnefoy
© Mercure de France, 1977

First published in English translation by Seagull Books, 2014
English translation © Beverley Bie Brahic, 2014

ISBN 978 1 8030 9 271 3

British Library Cataloguing-in-Publication Data
A catalogue record for this book is available from the British Library

Typeset by Seagull Books, Calcutta, India
Printed and bound by WordsWorth India, New Delhi, India

CONTENTS

TRANSLATOR'S ACKNOWLEDGEMENTS

I am grateful to the editors of the following journals where these translations first appeared: *PN Review* ('The Fit of Laughter'); *The Fortnightly Review* ('Egypt'); *The Hudson Review* ('Rue Traversière', 'Return, in the Evening', 'Second Rue Traversière').

EGYPT

I

There were a lot of us on that ship, adrift for days, all its engines and lights off, but propelled, one felt, by a hidden force that kept those of us aboard from feeling alarmed, if not exactly carefree. 'One', 'we', the others, I, were a group of friends, with many events in our common past, then during the first period of the voyage or the dream a thousand ups and downs, an abundance I still feel, that sense of a time truly lived. But this memory was being effaced, and it vanished completely with the final episode, right from the start, as if it were in its nature to unravel, without violence but for ever, something that the joys, preoccupations and lessons of a lifetime had brought to maturity.

A few certainties, all the same. It was summer, we were sailing the eastern Mediterranean, and although our voyage had no specific plan it began in Egypt, veered west, then pushed north towards shores I immediately felt would be mountainous.

One evening at nightfall, we arrived at a port whose houses, as it happened, staggered up the sides of a fairly high mountain, and even at times seemed to disappear in its folds. In this place, clearly, a major festival was drawing to a close; the streets were dotted with fires that mingled under the trees; the houses were open and glittered, and because of this it was easy to see that the higher-perched neighbourhoods were separated by stretches of woods or rock, bringing the hinterland down into the heart of the city almost. Here or there one made out among the roofs other dark spots, but these flickered phosphorescently—probably the site of churches. Another church, a sort of metropolis, sitting on a spur of land near the centre, its whole facade and the base of its great domes alight with a beautiful yellow light, looked down on the harbour in its entirety, and the whole of the bay—of all the places and monuments in this strange land the church was what one picked out from a distance. But it looked—was it just an illusion?—deserted, silent.

I was at the ship's prow among the passengers gathered there, indistinct already, whispering—and I wondered, 'Is this Salonica? Is this Smyrna?' not excluding that it might be an entirely different city, one I might never have heard of. My only conviction, whence a preference, but slight, for Salonica, was that this port slowly looming up faced south and backed onto a vast, almost empty, region that vanished into Asia's depths. But the ship was coming alongside the quay, with the same slowness and gentleness it had had these past few days, and already we were disembarking among the men and women who lingered on the shore even if here and there the sea breeze had started to lift and scatter—sparks of brightness under others dying down—the wilted flowers and a debris of garlands.

And I question, gaily at first, some of the passers-by I meet, 'What city is this?'

It's strange, they don't understand. Heads turn towards me, they smile, they've caught the sense of my words, I can see, the lack of understanding hasn't to do with language, and yet, more deeply, nothing registers. Suddenly anxious, I attempt to rephrase my question. For example, 'What do you call this place you live in?' Or, 'If you were outside the town, and coming back (I vaguely perceive a track along the sea, under the cliffs, with a donkey, and the city in the distance against the sun, now setting), you would tell me: I'm going to . . .?' But none of these stratagems evokes the least response. It seems that even the notion of name, or of place, is utterly foreign to these people, at least as far as their city is concerned. Moreover, they are hardly listening to me, we move apart, politely, and in the meantime my friends have scattered in the crowd.

II

I wake, and all day I can't stop thinking about the brightly lit city, the quay, the total incomprehension, with immense sadness and a feeling of solitude.

Then, that evening, the telephone rang, and I learnt what had happened during the previous night. My mother, who lived alone in the city where I was born, had had a stroke as she was going to bed; she'd spent the entire night and the following morning on the floor, almost unconscious—dreaming probably. I also learnt that she'd greeted her rescuers with the words of a diminished mind, the uncertain and whimsical perception of a child on the threshold of language, but with all her usual courtesy. She apologized for bothering so many people. She wanted, I believe, to offer them refreshments. I thought then, and not without sadness again, that always concealed beneath this courtesy, and even from herself, was the experience of a kind of distance: the people around her in this part of the country that she'd had to come to when she was young and spend her life in, remained foreign—cold, she used to say, distrustful, without the outgoingness and give-and-take she associated on the other hand, as its great virtue, with her place of birth, her father's native province.

Morning again, and I went to the station, early. A fine, crisp day, pale sunlight running across the surfaces of shadows that looked like water, shimmering. I saw a sort of little girl in jeans wandering along the quay, humming, her shadow falling on the pavement in two or three sharply curved lines that darted like birds; they seemed to me sentences, maybe rich with meaning. Sometimes, holding her right foot out gracefully in front of her in this game of black and white, she tested the ground as if it were thin ice, before putting her weight on it suddenly, laughing and tossing her head. Then she stopped, gazing off at I don't know what—nothing probably. And I understood—I too all of a sudden—that her name was *Egypt*. At this my spirits lifted, for I was no longer in the life where one feels sadness but back in the dream; and also because I understood perfectly that if the dream was starting up again now but in the places and situations of my waking life, in this country, here, where people and cities have names, it was closely related to this life, and it must therefore be a good dream. I boarded the train, once more in my life I looked at the quay; it was beginning to flow gently in the summer light, as if I were on a shore.

III

Once more in my life, and how many times! When I was a child, roughly the age of the little girl, I was in the other country, in the mountains, with the sun coming up behind on the left, the train that shot out from between the rocks on the right, rushed towards us with its brow unfurrowed, then was gone, splashing us with its shadow, scarcely broken between cars by the commas, the dots—or the words again? —of light. The whole village would go to the station early in the morning 'to watch the train go by'; would go back at the end of the afternoon to greet its return; my mother, my grandmother, my aunt, often traipsing along, in the idleness of summer, and sometimes we were the ones who climbed down the still-shuddering steps, with our holiday jumble of bags. Crushed by the long night spent in packed compart-ments and in two or three station buffets, brimming with unfinished dreams, flapping my wings like a dazzled owl, I saw clearly that they were all there together, the living and the dead! In the foreground, the held-out hands, the mous-taches, the chignons with steel knitting needles stuck in them, sun glinting on a holy-dove brooch pinned to a bodice, but off in the distance, smiling, anxious as in a photograph in its oval frame, those aged faces of which they'd later say,

'No, you couldn't have known him. No, he was no longer around . . .' And always the *Promé té ché*, also known as the madwoman, on the quay going from group to group in her great bouffant—but tattered and dusty black dress—coiffed one might have said with a huge basket of fruit and flowers, long since fresh. She would go up to everyone, she would even lean over me, laughing, wagging her finger as if in warning, jokingly, or recalling an old promise. 'Oh, I promise you . . .' she'd say, and you told yourself, or I ended up believing, that a fiancé had once left her here in this station and hadn't come back. Everyone was talking very loudly, of course, exclaiming, laughing, no one paid her the least attention, any more than to the shadow that crossed her face when the last train door slammed shut. After which, with the last of the voyagers, humming, a little apart, she returned to the village and you'd see her there at night still, squatting in her dark doorway, busy stirring the embers under some cast-iron pots. I loved her; to me it seemed she was the earth itself, the earth that I sensed, in the dying of villages, the last processions for good weather or rain, the last patois songs of the goose-girls in the meadows, was growing old aphasic. And I dreamt that one day I would—but how?—right the wrong done by the fiancé who had fled in the morning of the world.

THE FRUIT

The sun might have been unbearable. But its glare was somehow checked by a wall one only glimpsed through the foliage—motionless, the leaves hanging, and in peace, on the shoreless afternoon.

Silence, for a good while. After which she appeared at the top, not without effort—you felt this at the end, you might say she clawed at holes that weren't holes, round crumbling protuberances; all the same, she was laughing —and perched on the edge, tossing her thin legs over the top rather gracelessly; a sort of little girl whose face, in this gold light, seemed a silver disk, and even very smooth, a little dull.

She laughed again, maybe because in her skirt that made a pocket over her knees she had fruit from the nearby trees, which she took and ate. Fat cherries that held the sun on their far sides. A bottomless supply, maybe too much, the fruit slid from the bright fabric, slid and fell with a muffled thump into the grass of the end of the world.

THE FIRES

The boat glides down canals which open, endlessly it seems, into other canals, all of them in all directions lined with rather high walls, some two metres of smoothly fitted stones beneath leaves stirring in a breeze. The day is over, and the water begins to reflect the rays of a huge sinking sun, hidden at times, though for now rarely, by the walls on either side.

The boatman has lit a fire, in the bow.

Here, at water level, is a doorway closed by a grille, children leaning against it from the inside, laughing, their foreheads fringed with brown hair. Visible between their narrow shoulders, barely covered by painted fabrics, a big garden where other fires, made of grass, burn; a garden in which many birds sing and flit in bright bunches across the patch of sky cut out by the doorway. The boat is chained to a mole now. Its fire gives off masses of vibrant, hot air.

We wait. Nothing will become any longer in the unmoving brightness. Only the slapping of the water will stop and start against the hull. The children's laughter the last colour flaring up here or there in the dusk of flowers, fruit, like time's remainder, which evaporates.

A CUPOLA

We'd decided—stupidly? not completely, no—to paint a sort of cupola. There it was, up above us in the afternoon heat, a white hollow, not quite smooth, beyond a little narthex, itself utterly white and naked—all there was to see there was a statue of the Virgin halfway up, with its branch from another year, and the paint pots and our brushes, brought in just before dawn.

·

And we were beginning to paint, laughing and bumping against one another, up on our ladders, for space was cramped between the four walls, yet we each had our share of the image to paint—some vague, tall, gesticulating figure to extract from the red, the ochre and the blue, to merge with the gestures of the other bodies and faces, towards the calm eye at the top of the stones, so that everything was running together, brushes crossing, haloes shimmering on top of one another and gazes that began appearing in the trees—palm trees, lots of palm trees, against a setting sun—faces laughing, rising like moons. As we went we effaced, we started over, the cricket singing outside, indifferent, *'ingénu'*,[1] in the branch beneath the Virgin.

O beautiful afternoon in the stillness of the heat!

In which, all the same, we had to work fast, too fast, for all these brushes banging together, amazed, dripped paint over our bodies, splattering them, making one of us red and the other blue, or brown, and all of us signs shimmering from so much sun up under the vault, in the silence. And because at the same time, strangely, night was falling. And because the girl of the statue, who was painting with us or was being painted, we no longer knew which, the eternal Virgin, the star on her forehead, wanted to go home and slid down the ladder, dress tucked under her knees and crossed back through the antechamber, its blue turning mauve like the evening hills. She was running off now, she was calling. One of us, this time or another, was there to chase her, to catch up with her; and with a bound then she threw herself into the thick grass, knees drawn up under her chin, eyes closed, suddenly calm.

ROME, THE ARROWS

I

I have entered and now I'm going around rooms with large paintings and fresco fragments on their walls. All these works are manifestly superb; their dense, bright colours rise like warm air above grass fires on fine September mornings and their forms vibrate, though this shimmering doesn't signify anything unreal; on the contrary, what emanates from them is a robust joy, a faith, as if, having been washed of its shadows —shadows that one might say turn around something fixed: a hinge, a hidden door?—the earth breathed more easily. But in these *Visitations* set against a backdrop of mountains, *Nativities* with innumerable wise men dotted among the trees, in which, star notwithstanding, it could be day or night, these *Baptisms*, these pages from the lives of the saints where, in the vibration, a bit of red flame flickers—and how many other subjects only dimly known to me, though not entirely foreign, subjects I feel sure I would understand if I didn't have to go around so quickly—what strikes me most is the unique use made of perspective. It is rigorously centred as its great Tuscan inventors, and amateurs of geometry wished, and yet it isn't.

At the very moment the eye, pulled towards the vanishing point, is about to rest in the lines' convergence, a convergence that brings the coherence of the meaning to maturity, an irresistible force draws it towards another centre, although— how to put this?—the gesture of departure is annulled even as it is accomplished, whence the feeling that the new vanishing point is both very distant from the first and very close, and that this kind of infiniteness can only spring from the calm heart of unity. Historians and art critics, have you tried to *see*, I mean to follow in its duration, in its apparent hesitation, the arrival at the target of arrows shot by the eternal archer, the Zen master, from far away, unseen by us, invisible? They lodge around the centre, then along comes an arrow that strikes a little off to the side; and we sense that what we have here is neither an effect of clumsiness nor of supreme skill, in irony, but a hint, we don't yet know of what, proffered in indifference and in peace; and meanwhile, the last arrow comes along and takes its place as expected beside the first ones. Looking at all this, two thoughts came to me. The first was a memory of Plotinus, who teaches that the One is above all categories of being; and suggests that perspective, which is a fact at the level of being, gives but a metaphorical image of the idea of the centre, whence, of course, important effects on the work, unconscious or not, of artists. Some of them, for example, dimly aware of this character of exile, can have concluded that any work involving perspective must know itself to be an image, content or not with itself; while others . . . Might one not conceive that there were, at least in the realm of the possible, painters who experimented with perspective, an arrow heavily feathered with the colours and lights of the world which flings itself out of what is towards— towards what? let's say what is not—that which lifts us up and carries us along, and finds itself in the absence of knowledge; and takes fire then, up there, sometimes?

But already, the other memory, ordinary memory, was falling over this somewhat confused glimpse, and brought with it, not more clarity but more enigma, almost an anguish. I should say that these paintings had from the start astonished me, less for their still-considerable strangeness than for something on the contrary very familiar, intimately bound up with them, like a thread among others in a weft. And when I thought of Plotinus my still-blurred recollection grew precise. 'But of course,' I exclaimed (to myself), 'the painter whose echo, even direct influence, I feel here is Piero della Francesca! He too painted bright colours, though without this kind of supreme ease that one feels is only allotted to beings more angelic (or more earthly) than we are. And he too understands—though on a single plane, let's say that of measure, of number, whereas how many others there are here!—the dialectic of the centre and the off-to-the-side, of symmetries troubled by dissymmetries.' Piero was helping me decipher the unknown paintings; in a sense, he was explaining them to me. But, oddly, far from rendering them more natural and thus linking them to some Italian region or historical period, the quality in Piero that lent itself to parallels and to meaning was rendered incomprehensible by the comparison. To be frank, *The Flagellation*, for example, or *The Baptism of Christ*, had already struck me, had *also* struck me for something in them that the Italian tradition failed to explain, and even for something in them that is absent from everything, absent, if I may say so, from the world, something in their nonetheless very dense presence, so rustic, so promptly at ease with a reflection of sky in a puddle of water or a bird hopping about. And it is this syncope of the background, this absolute heterogeneity of what should have existed as the warmest, the most natural background that was growing now in my memory, illuminating the works of the master of Borgo San Sepolcro[2] and at the same time dulling them the way a flash of lightning can drain the colour from a summer or autumn morning over the grass fires. Piero wasn't reducing the disparity, wasn't bringing me closer to the Orient towards which the vast waters of the unknown 'school' rolled, he was himself being swept away.

II

And I went around these rooms, so many of them, as if this museum—for surely I was in a museum—were one of the grandest in this Italy I couldn't place, one of those museums that don't merely house, as so many do, the works of the local *cultura*, but have, over centuries, collected a real civilization's necessarily diverse offerings. In their unity, which struck me right away and which was still remarkable, not just for its stylistic elements but as a deep interior locus where these signs became act, and this art a religion, I began to perceive the diffractions, the nuances—on some level almost the oppositions—which reflected the great variables of the psyche, or of flesh-and-blood existence: one or other painting seeming, in its supreme effortlessness, at times a trifle stiff, in the manner of the Primitives, another a touch mannered. True, an entire people had experienced all this, and suffered, in return for its quest of the good, the shocks of matter's irreducibility, and history's as well. And I ask, 'But what is this? Here is a society which must have had its architecture and its poets: How can we be in the dark about so many testimonies?

And how is it that these paintings, enough of them to add a whole new Italy to our Italy, have such an inner relationship with it—especially with the late Trecento and early Quattrocento—in their differences that I feel them both of that moment, that place, which are our past, and outside it, in some future, albeit a timeless one?'

And I asked myself again, 'And how does it happen that I feel so sure, however disheartening this feeling may be, that I will never understand the exact nature of the relationship between these works I see so vividly here—I who love painting —and the art of Tuscany or the Marches that I've known for so long? It's as if I couldn't even locate the object of my concern in my mind. As if, in sum, these great retables that surround me—invitation, entreaty, solicitude, presence—as if they were, in the end, only the final screen that prevents me seeing the face of what most concerns me. I see the red, yes, the bright yellow, the cold blue, and the flowery bouquet, still a little snowy, of green and rose and violet, I feel the wind that bends them, but there is also, I know, in this brazier an image, oh not formal, no, not coloured—smoke gives us glimpses of such things, in the morning, or the smell of the incense one burns—and this image which would be the revelation escapes me. The clearer one sees, the sharper one suffers from the effects of the blind spot. The more one advances—and I have advanced, I know I have—the keener one's awareness that a door will stay shut. What is this art of peace and cruelty? Where, oh where am I?'

And someone walking beside me responds, 'Oh, come on! These are just the paintings that might have been painted in Rome, in the days Giotto, Duccio, Pietro Cavallini and some other young followers were laying the foundations of a new art, *un art nouveau*, as you say in your part of the world, had the Curia not left Rome for Avignon.

'Don't you see? Rome's entire past, so eloquent in its ruins, in all its theological and ritualistic means, its riches and its poverty, predisposed it to lead the revival of Italian art, to become the command centre already foretold by the uncertain and nascent technique of perspective—and along comes an accident of history to rob it of the handful of patrons and the crowds it needed for this sort of fire to take! Isn't that a reason to grow feverish over what might have been? A reason for an unhappy adolescent to be filled, rent with visions, heartsick in the empty rooms, on the marble-strewn hills? And a reason for regret when, in the fifteenth and sixteenth centuries, the opportunities return, art starts up again, but slowly, influenced by other schools—too late? Here you have what might have been beautiful and good in our city; or if you prefer, what was, what for ever remains: the immense frustration that troubled Raphael and exasperated Michelangelo, that marred with its discouraged impatiences, its lassitudes our stupid *fa presto*, and perhaps haunts all modern art—yes Tiepolo, yes, Delacroix, yes, Turner—and was only somewhat calmed for an hour I shall call autumnal—the ripe fruit but not the flower, not alas the vivid greenness—in the great baroque dreams. Oh, signore, absolute art was once possible. At the one point where the lessons of Eastern and Western antiquity converged: where the lesson of time—chance—was coming to maturity in ruined palaces; where that of charity proposed by the Church in the catacombs was kept alive by the candles flickering on the mosaics of apses—yes, this quality of absoluteness but negative, soon disembodied, the agape of the Christians, and glory's possibilities, sensuous storms that the other name of Rome evokes, weren't they going to lead, all at once, in the positive absolute forever dreamt of and never yet attained, to images of standing figures, works one would visit laughing as at a festival—lead, yes, in an explosion of fireworks and rockets, to an end of history? Among your painters only one had some experience, from the very beginning, of this positivity that was our ultimate good here: Piero della Francesca. Is this because he came from the borderlands, the hill countries where something of the two traditions must have survived, like grasses mingling with other grasses at the ends of ploughed fields? Be that as it may, you are familiar with the transparency of his colours, the music of his forms, his tranquil assurance; you even evoked this humour of his, in which the pains and regrets that usually compose your "great art" seem to fade. And it's true that the positive is in him subdued, even somnolent—it's his peasant ways, he takes a siesta, he's a bit of a sleepwalker—still, your Piero belongs to us, which is a consolation: it gives us a touch of hope. One can, we may agree, conceive that the *Madonna della Misericordia*'s way of holding her head, in Borgo, or the *Madonna del Parto* above all (the angels' socks, those four colours set free to chirp on the ground!—such apparitions, such fancifulness!)—are a point of contact between you and us and, why not, a door? You are walking in the deserted countryside one August afternoon, preoccupied—suddenly you see you've been following a wall and there's this low door . . .'

'But where am I?' I said again. 'Say what you like, you exist. Or if not you, these works of art. In at least one sense, I can see them.'

'You are in Rome, of course. You thought there was just one Rome? Didn't you understand the lesson of the arrows coming from God knows where to hit the target here or there? Rome is the centre, therefore it is everywhere. Rome is one, therefore it is multiple. And since it has a history . . .

See, everything is here! In fact, *the popes never left Rome.* There was no Avignon. Art, the great art the West was hoping for, the art of place and formula, had its place and its formula here[3]—I don't say now—and what you call your artistic past, from 1309 on, is mere myth, it didn't exist, except, that is, for Piero, though you see him differently from us, and Domenico Veneziano. The art happened, we are saved, my friend. And that's why you who aren't do not even perceive our existence.'

III

'True,' I say sadly. 'But I've looked so hard! In Rome and far from Rome. In lit sanctuaries and modest mountain chapels. During the opening hours of museums and through doors left ajar in churches converted to garages. When the sun rises on Umbria, and when night falls.'

'But you only looked at colour and form. Haven't you noticed, those are the only words in your critical vocabulary. Oh, a few images interested you but only for what they try to say. You have to look at the spaces between things, my dear fellow traveller. You have to sense, instinctively, that what was under your eyes in those countries of yours is never anything but a grille, something achieved, done, bearing the seal of finitude, which if need be gives you access to a text—whereas by removing the grille, forgetting the message idea and thinking of simultaneity, if you can't grasp the absolute you will at least achieve the full page. Wait! Let's lay a grille over this page! Imagine mildness, for instance, but without cruelty; or the one with the other, yes, all right, but without the serenity, without the innocence. And look, this painting. You see, your usual Italy . . .'

'Indeed,' I say. 'Botticelli's *Pieta* in the Fogg Museum.'

'. . . is simply a case in point, in our art! Except, as I feared, and to your credit, the veil is askew, a drop of the infinite still trickles in. Never mind! You know it all now. You and your painters, strange mortal beings who detest your finitude, but so clumsily, so attached, in fact, to your limits, you are, each of you, the sentences; and us, teeming, the words. You, speaking, are matter; and we, in our silence, spirit. That's why, even when you wander through what they call Rome, all you bring with you is absence. When you look at Rome, except for a peak or two, sticking up here and there—yes, there are some—you don't know how to see us out on the edges holding out our arms to you nonetheless, clothed in marble, that is to say, lightning, against the real sky. Oh, my friend! We are there, all the same, we watch over you. We live on your street, in your house, even in your gestures. We speak to one another about you, in front of you, in you. Lay your hand on this table, on that sheet of paper—and this city that opens, these coppery facades near the sea, the gold of puddles on the pavement after rain, the dim arrivals, and the moments of bliss, the heart-breaking horizons at your windows, are us. And our paintings, our statues—for we make such things, you see them, it's as if we lifted a curtain to go into another room, and our friends are there, in the endless thickets of images—they teem within yours, since at a single point in any work of art—what pessimism, your Euclidean geometry, what an abdication, that perspective of yours—each line has countless perpendiculars, a true sun, where you see only one, death.'

'You are the sum,' I say, 'and we . . . What was it our master used to say?[4] The abolition!'

'We are much more than the sum! And you have no idea what your exclusives reject. From our least branch hang clusters of worlds. Your contradictions unravel, your aporias, your miseries dissipate in the skies, in the drifting of lights. What naivety, that roll-of-the-dice business. Your poet conceived of the whole but we think of the One beyond, another density of the infinite, where simplicity begins. Let yourself sink, yes, but feel the surge from below that lifts you, my son. Accept! Recognize the foothills of the true country. See, already, the rose and the green of this aroma in the grasses on the rocky outcrop, this nothing—the simple gesture, the peals of laughter.'

'Yes, I know our rites are not—how shall I put it—sufficiently powerful.'

'Then enter, the way you've done so often, this chapel of the fields, listen to the silence vibrate in thousands of cicada and grasshopper songs, look at this *Madonna.*'

I looked up at the old fresco, so marred, so fragmented by the cracks in the eroded colours and forms that the ruin, in this instant before its utter effacement, seemed to have changed sign, to blaze out, to be a kind of writing in the writing. And between the face of the young woman bending down and the face of the laughing child holding out its arms, its gaze, its mouth, it seemed to me the one's laughter and the other's smile multiplied like the sun in a mirror, like a thousand suns launched by a thousand mirrors, a thousand boats each of which had crossed the still-deep-red horizon, climbed to the zenith and was going down over vast ploughed fields but already being reborn in each fold of colour, in each of the form's hollows, shining, cruel—when the mirror turned, darting sun into our eyes—but with what excruciating gentleness. Infinity moving blindingly over the shore's foam, yes, that was you! Egypt that shimmers endlessly in the rapid water of the world, you again! Other words, so many of them, visible in the name of Rome, again you! And without composing sentences, in the instant's immensity, I perceived in a single glance, I effaced a thousand former labyrinths—understanding for a start that as we wandered through Avignon or elsewhere in human history's certainly endless pain the genius of time and place had matured for us, from one word to the next had been caught in the fire and kept available for use, and now offered us what? what our gods above had promised in vain, the verb, the word, the ripe cluster.

Simultaneously, however, I had to acknowledge another more complex thought: which was, first of all, that I felt time passing—streaming by, shall we say, rather than lapping in peace, whitening against the shore rocks—and this thought couldn't help but affect the art I'd been given a glimpse of, without diminishing the infiniteness of its profound exchanges, which were growing stormy; I saw black where I now sensed the imminence of lightning, huge opaque downpours over bleached mountains. Art (I see no other word) was again mingling with the divine; and an increasing baroque was about to rend with its feverish movements what had for an instant on its four twisted columns been the uncreated, the positive, the simple fire—while something primitive, still a trifle stiff, its bravely delineated contours spread over swaths of ochre and blue, *precipitated* into this troubled solution, like a will striving to separate itself from the passions, from vain ambitions, dreams, so as to begin over again in deprivation the surely reasonable act of wisdom. And I, fascinated, 'rigid as an extravagant',[5] watched these dissociative movements closely, I pursued them into the image's eddies, whereas it might perhaps have sufficed (and I thought it!) to ignore them— yes, I recognized (shall we say I even sought to distinguish, with a bitter joy?) these 'styles' as we also say, these moments of the mind we had decided were incompatible and which, certainly, as soon they slipped from the unity—where they still glowed before me—really are . . . Why on earth must we always fall back on thinking we are dreaming when perhaps we just are? Thinking that it is our arm in the water that makes the lights move? And why does the shadow of a memory fall so quickly over this revelation? For I have already seen, not just this face—Oh Isis, mother, it's all too natural —but this image.

God! Now it seemed I was in Monterchi chapel one summer morning gazing at the great fresco that tells of a life to be born,[6] that tempers with irony, wisdom and peace what we know remains the finite, the not-divine, in the infinity, the divinity of what is to be born.

And I went on walking, in the night. Bent over, the coil of waxed hemp around my arm, at my fingertips the little flame.[7] And around me and endless the rock, now and then lit by a few remnants of paint.

To write, to publish this account, this memento of my travels,[8] still in the dark about the fate of *The Flagellation* and *The Madonna of Senigallia!*[9] Not only have we lost, for ever perhaps, two great works of art, the theft has also destroyed the feeling of presence[10]—place and sense indivisible—characteristic of the Palace of Urbino and the Piero paintings. Why, I'll not attempt to say, but this architecture and this painting breathed with the same distant respiration, came towards us with the same ecstasy. So once again in these strange years—beguiled by images, yet iconoclastic—we must resign ourselves to the knowledge that the evidence of Oneness, where here and there it still keeps watch, does not with all its majesty know how to halt the twilight hand that hurries history on.

Convenerunt in unum was once written under *The Flagellation.* What sort of mind could have selected these words, taken from a passage in the *Psalms* about kings and princes, Christ's adversaries? 'They leagued themselves against him,' the lost inscription said. And I, who was tempted to read: 'They came together as one.'

An empty room in a chateau whose music we no longer hear except in gusts, whose very peace is like a further wound, is now in its shadowy afternoon the altar towards which all hope of meaning turns, all thought of *place*, the sole value we can erect against the drift of the *signs*. Don't, please—if not the heavens, at least the line of the hills under the wide clear sky around Urbino—let the museum's conservators replace the missing paintings by others, don't let them use art history to palliate the absence of the painting that seemed to want to force, in peace, a passage through writing's labyrinth; and gave so profoundly, so lastingly, the impression of having succeeded.

An empty room. The absence that still resembles life, like a call: the trace of a presence that once existed and might again exist on the horizon of that which—signifying without signifier, sign without referent, tongue without speech—flows from everywhere, rolls in vain.

Shall we be forced, more and more often, to *dream* what *was*? Visitors to the ducal palace not finding what they sought —some for years like the star. Others travel ashamed through famished nations, dismembered civilizations. And all of us soon constrained to dream even the earth, its plants and animals, this great art lost for ever, roads, unable to do anything for the few true countries that remain intact. Nothing is lost,

I know, there will always be the photograph of the once-sacred valleys, of rooms humans and the divinity once shared, even the clump of absolute grass on the threshold of a mountain hut; and look, here's a child, smiling: who knows to whom, or where it was, or when, but how dense this air, this real place! For a while longer there'll be chamois or ibex in the reserves, retables of Quattrocento altars in the museums of everywhere—once I enjoyed these exiles, but that was fifteen years ago,[11] when the essential was still in place. From each of these wreckages, however, something crumbles, invisible, that in its original place was a reason to be, a hope.

And I confess I tell myself—such is the need for hope—that, who knows, perhaps this generalization of the dream state was necessary, this extension of a state whose riches are as great as its yet-unfathomed possibilities; so that the good, which we have never approached in our long nocturnal history, except in dreams, may flare up like a surprising second fire in this world moving towards its end. Unity, the breath of Presence in communities, in works: so much bad faith in each of us is forever destroying these things; perhaps it is right that this wind from everywhere blow till it becomes pure blackness, so that in this spreading void the idea of place establish itself, both of the unreal, henceforth, and of a way of thinking rediscovered, freed, an intuition that one can at last experience in a surge of joy as if one were oneself the lightning? To found, to create, to give meaning as we would offer a glass of water to strangers, this never seemed so natural, was never so simple as in the desert. I 'think' therefore that when some hope, some work admits its defeat, falls apart, true form is revealed. I dream of another earth, appearing by degrees—vaster trees loaded with fruit, swiftly moving clouds bright again, meadows 'dotted with flowers', as we used to say, and the chapels of the fields, in the morning, with their paintings, those that are as simple as roads winding through grass—as the fire that will have burnt this one dissipates.

How beautiful this earth was, all the same! But there was a black spot in the animals' leaping, a thorn in the bouquets: the mother we didn't know how to love properly, with abandon, whence the languages, the history, the art too, thought, all this abstraction, this feverishness in the enigma, the enthusiasm that rends things! The other earth will be the daughter who runs ahead of us into the day she gives birth to as she goes—laughing as she picks the berries, singing as she bites into the fruit.

CREST

The notion of a red that might be blue, of an exterior that might be interior, of an all of that which might be a body that hands, of an unknown kind, might nail sweating to cushions of shadow, flew past gracefully and came to perch on a stone, crest in the cool air.

THE GODS

We stood, with the masons, on the highest terrace towards the end of an autumn afternoon. Suddenly 'it' rose out of the ravine and poured past as if summoned to the east—clusters of vibrant wings and shadows of bodies, translucid, swirling, thousands and thousands of them in the midst of other clusters. What silence, until night fell! The workers were done, no bird sang, no insect hummed, we watched these great wheels expand and contract, some of them so thick they dimmed the sun.

Now and again one of these travellers would swoop to the parapet or our still-bright sleeves; and we told ourselves its heart was beating, we liked that the delicately wrought ancient face shone in the infinitesimal, under a tiara.

THE PRAGUE DISCOVERIES

2 May 1975

As faithfully as possible, the moments of one of those reveries that now and then form within us, just as the other kind of dream, the night-time kind, form and dissolve.

Brief prose texts I've been writing lately, also dreamlike, which must owe something of their intimacy to the unconscious, for I try not to let my reflections control whatever surprising, incomprehensible thing pops up. It seems to me that I am able to perceive what the secret parcel of life that appears under my pen already has of the organic and the specific; and that I can therefore help it grow and breathe by prudent pruning obedient only to the text's needs. Which amounts to thinking, let me say in passing, that André Breton was wrong to consider absolute automatism the condition of true speech. Everything one's most recent memories throw up, everything the eye catches or the ear is subjected to can enter unhindered, without the juxtapositions, measurement, careful weighings that any attempt at formulation, even without the mind's conscious approbation, entails. Crossing out, on the other hand, choosing while letting the other choose, facilitates an economy, encourages a deposit—who knows? incites the underlying thought to use this first rapid jotting down of one's thoughts as an opportunity for further composition by means of which, in certain works of poetry or in the arts, meaning brings peace, and music. Already in what we spontaneously call 'good dreams' this deeper work has taken place, thanks to which a form, heard in the élans of desire, can be freed and rise to the light, but to wait for it—this desire—to receive it, refresh it with its water, soothe it with its serious joy.

Les beaux rêves . . . Just as surrealism was wrong to rush words' already impatient course, to prohibit stopping at what might be the crossroads, the short cut, the lost dwelling's threshold—yes, who knows? and why suppress the one big question—so psychoanalysis' understanding of desire would be impoverished if it didn't, in giving an 'aesthetic' dimension to its study of symbols, try to appreciate the elements of composition, rhythm, silence, rustlings in the margins—of *beauty*—which can put an unforgettable face on the scenes we traverse in our sleep.

But in what I mean to recount today, the reverie occurred unprompted, beyond the white page, beyond any project to experiment or to write, even rapidly, I'd say irresistibly until an interruption, without knowing whether this interruption was the end or an encounter with some obstacle. In the event I only listened, and I only want now, years later, to remember situations and questions engraved at that time in my memory. Of course, my writing is going to modify the details, whether for or against whatever was seeking itself there on a suddenly favourable occasion—believing myself faithful, I will not be *attentive* in the way I spoke of earlier. For the essential, however, I believe I am a serious witness, and merely a witness.

~

In the beginning, a brief newspaper item. In Prague Castle, I read, a room had been walled up and forgotten for centuries; one day someone detected its presence, opened it up and found it filled with paintings, including a good-sized Rubens collected in the seventeenth century by a prince who had himself perhaps hidden the paintings.

And immediately, this 'idea for a story', but so urgent, as I said, and so prompt to reveal itself that right away nothing else matters. A number of clues—I won't try to know which—made them think that there were some sixteenth- and seventeenth-century paintings very close by, in an underground room previously thought to be half filled with stones. They extract many of these huge blocks. They see another door, which they open and now there's a staircase whose steps are missing. A historian is charged with an initial reconnaissance. Still, if they give him the lamp and a rope, it's mostly due to his own impatience, which is beyond reason and astonishing —the stomping of a beast warned of some presence.

Down he goes, and spends half an hour or so in what one imagines to be a room or passageway. Then he tugs on the rope, they pull him up, and here he is, pale, while below him and thundering, at length, God! the roar of an avalanche, the falling, apparently, of countless other stones. What happened, what did he see? To begin with and for some time he doesn't answer, then he states, his eyes wandering, or lowered, that nothing happened, he saw nothing. The paintings? No, there are no paintings. In any case, no one conceives of going back down, no, nor to look again for these canvases, for what just fell swept away and destroyed everything. This he is sure of. How can he be so sure? You might think he wanted this to happened, that he caused it! someone is already insinuating. Again he doesn't answer, his eyes elsewhere. Obviously the question was absurd.

So the day passes, and the historian goes home with a young woman, his friend, to his house off in the mountains, which overlooks a meadow dotted with flowers. She, still looking a little astonished, not saying much—this is her way of swimming through the water of days, sparkling, rapid—

yes, she was there that morning, in front of the walled-up door, and since then she has been troubled. What happened is beyond any conceivable explanation, she feels—and yet she wants to know. All day long she has, therefore, with looks, invited him to confide in her but in vain. No denial on his part, no impatience, no, his face is closed, his eyes troubled. Now it is night, and despite the window open to the stars, and his nearness on the bed on which they have both lain down, she no longer sees his face, he can only sense her hand in the shadows, taking his—is this why? in any case, he speaks. Let's say he returns with a murmured allusion—what allusion I don't know—to the edge of the space that, since the morning, his silence has kept at bay, sealed off; and she, fast: 'Tell me? I feel sure you saw something.'

To which, equally fast, very low (the window is to his right, you can hear the breeze, the sky is calm): 'Yes, the paintings,' he answers.

'The paintings! But why on earth didn't you say something?'

'I was afraid.'

~

'Afraid, my friend? Afraid of what?'

'I don't know. Of the paintings . . . no, not the paintings.'

It's a strange voice he has now, as if broken, as if resigned, but also at times feverish and occasionally exalted, explaining, chaotically, he was afraid, and is still afraid, God knows! No, not of the paintings, with them, rather. Or with others, 'that we both know, my friend.' But afraid of the paintings too, yes, all the same. Afraid of them above all.

'But why?'

'Because they were . . . different.'

A word that incites the avowal she alone could have provoked, because of how she looks straight ahead, her silences, and because of her voice, it too hesitant, stopping and starting up again. He is going to speak, he will even want to say everything, he will suffer not to be able to say everything, say all of it.

~

'Different? What do you mean? Unexpected?'

'Oh, yes!'

'How, unexpected? In what way?'

'I can't say.'

'And that's what's frightening? The unexpectedness?'

'Yes.'

'That's all?'

'No.'

~

'But in what way were they different? The paintings? Tell me. Was it the subjects?'

'Oh no, no.'

'The subjects were familiar? Which subjects?'

'I don't know. The usual. Some *Visitations*, some *Magi*. Mythological scenes. Portraits. As everywhere.'

'So was it the style? An unknown school?'

'No, oh no.'

'But what school was it? You must know, since it was familiar.'

'Yes. Some Florentines, especially. A lot of Florentine painting.'

'Which period?'

'The seventeenth century. Yes, above all. Some from before that. A lot of seventeenth-century work.'

'But don't you know that school of painting well?'

'Oh, God, yes!'

'So how could it be so surprising? Was it other painters? Ones you didn't know?'

'No.'

'You recognized them all?'

'Yes, no, I'm not sure. I didn't have time to see everything. Anyway that's not the question.'

'Give me names.'

'Cigoli, Giovanni da San Giovanni . . . But others. Even some Venetians, I believe. And the Rubens. But mostly Florence. And again, let me tell you, this is not important. That's not . . .'

'But what, what?'

(Now she is pleading. She fears losing the contact.)

~

'I told you, they were—how did I put it?—*different*. Other.'

'But how, please tell me, how? The details? The expressions?'

'Nothing in particular.'

'Go on. Was it the colour?'

'Oh, what an idea! The colour . . . no.'

'Can you describe these canvases?'

'That would . . . It wouldn't get us anywhere. The difference is not something you can describe. It's not a question of words.'

'Why?'

'Because words are going to be *our* words, don't you see?'

~

'But you have something in mind right now, don't you? You see something?'

'Yes.'

'What? Say it fast, really fast!'

'Oh, nothing. An *Annunciation* perhaps.'

'Good. And then? Is it to do with the Virgin Mary? The angel?'

'It's the vase, too, and the flower.'

'What kind of flower? Unknown . . .' (All of a sudden she shivers, she feels cold.)

'None of that. The usual flower. Different, yes, but not in the sense you are thinking. Understand. Understand. It was what you'd expect in the way of paintings. Not an unknown kind of Cigoli, or Rubens, an unfamiliar period of their painting, for instance. Everything there, believe me, I could have dated to within two years. And not another nature, no, it was the same flowers and the same trees, and not another theology, either. And not even other faces, other looks. But it was . . . *other*.'

~

'Other—you mean, monstrous?'

'Not that, no. You're mistaken. No, not that.'

'So, more . . . an excess of beauty? Of purity? Something terrible from too much beauty, too much purity?'

'No.'

'I'm so afraid!'

'Listen!'

He's propped up on his elbow now, there in front of her, who sees the sky above him, around him, outside the big window on their right.

'Listen . . . it's as if . . . as if I had to understand suddenly that everything we have here in the way of painting, all these paintings from the past, and even from the recent past, yes, even Delacroix, even Cézanne—didn't exist, had never existed, were only an illusion.'

'But we have them, those paintings! Some of them are here in this house, close to us.'

'True. But they've always been under our eyes. So they are our dream. They are what we are. Whereas these others, their difference is that they've been lost, all of them together, because they've remained, how to put this, let me see, among themselves, in the past. The past is *other*.'

And again this feeling of not knowing how to be clear, to articulate.

'Listen. It's as if all of a sudden you realized that our languages . . . Yes, the words we use, the syntax, well, it wasn't even a language, it was . . . nothing, it was nothing, froth.[12] Froth moving under the star.'

'And them?'

'Them? Us? The star. No, not the star. The stones.'

~

She weeps.

And he, bent over her, looking at her, sees her again at certain moments in the past, and yesterday; he recognizes her.

'I tell you—it didn't surprise me.'

'God, who are you?

'Let me tell you—there were days when I almost knew. As a child, yes, as an adolescent. Looking at landscapes, mythological scenes, questioning cloud, naked flesh glowing in the semi-dark. All evidence is an enigma! All plentitude is barred with a pale line, closed around itself, that we no longer see, but which, now and then, zigzags across the wheat of the image—yes, across the mountains, the bodies—and bleaches the colour from everything, my friend, like lightning. We stitch these tatters, these colours, these signs, back together. But underneath, in the abyss . . .'

'The sky? The stones?'

'I called that night.'

She weeps. The task is there, ahead of her. All the days of a whole life stretched out like a road through flowers, birdsong, shadows. The sound of water, dazzled, troubled, the sound of footsteps over stones. And through the window, which is open—why?—already all those stars wrapped in the haze of the Milky Way—and something like a form breathing in this mist. Dawn is going to appear soon, however, like the dispersal of the images.

4 May

To this 'transcription' I must add two remarks—for the moment.

First, I haven't really done what I set out to do. In the dialogue especially, I've added more than the few details I'd initially planned. Nothing that hinders the movement, I think —the sense, if there is one, shouldn't be affected. All the same, so many of the words, in the figure the story makes, point to simmerings where other figures are already pressing in. Who said the retelling of a dream is without value, inadmissible, because it replaces the multiple with the definite? Each sentence is a labyrinth, everywhere we see grottoes where water gleams on stones. And in fact, noting the same memory two or four years ago—as I said, it's very old—I might easily have used many of the same words already, like the 'meadows dotted with flowers', which come from the original dictation; still, I couldn't have ended up with the day before yesterday's text.

The other remark—since the whole of this piece of writing, despite the real difference in time, came into being very quickly, almost without any crossing out, I must consider these few pages, relative as they may be, a finished text, in which the reverie is for ever fixed. And what I must emphasize now is that I am not without regret for the possibilities thus abolished, whether they were variations or new themes: so much so that I wonder what would have happened if I'd used this 'idea of a story' to really write one, with all the surplus description and fictional developments that the initial givens perhaps required—and would in that case have furnished. After all, the writing clearly indicated that it was an 'idea', a point of departure—that could have led to more substance. And who knows whether, taking truth as a pretext, feigning to believe that the initial reverie was valid in itself, I wasn't trying to close a door as the 'historian' in Prague Castle did? How, for example, might the presence of the 'young woman' have been fleshed out? And the house in the mountains? Very often the writing is just a seal one affixes to a threshold—even if the seal has the radiant shape of an open threshold.

This act of closure I may, however, use as a threshold—all I need to do is break with its structure, align myself from the outset with the simmerings, or shimmerings I spoke of, and add the associations it awakes in me, like so many unsounded facts. So our friend, the reader of cards, lays other cards over the first card she turned up.

And it is in this spirit that I shall now evoke—in haste, I will come back—another 'idea for a story' that came to me two days ago while I was writing, growing more and more insistent as I transcribed my phantasm and distanced myself from the point at which this idea could have been inserted.

What brought it to mind, I think, was that scene with a group of men and women peering down into an underground passage. At that point, it crossed my mind that this room below them, buried in the bowels of the earth, might all the same receive some light from a bay—one among others, so many others, on one of the castle's outside walls. Specifically, I saw a high sun-splashed wall, with dozens of windows at various levels, opening, of course, into rooms or banal passageways: but one of these, forgotten by everyone, and impossible to situate, would have been that of the buried room—yes, despite the window's being located at this or that floor, up in the light. What a contradiction! And what glimpses, in this fearfulness, of the workings of thought, its matter, when one is brought face to face with this evidence! Perhaps one member of the group, as they were peering at the rope, ought to have voiced this hypothesis, if not reported the reasoning that invited them to do so.

A lit wall! Those closed-up windows—for many of the rooms, known or unknown, have been long deserted—on that castle wall which is turned towards God-knows-what horizon, what night, in the vast silent countryside. And perhaps I as a child, visiting some chateau of the Loire, and looking from the embrasure of one wing onto the alternating rows of stone and panes gently blazing back at the evening sky. In the vast salons, the bedrooms, the small wood-panelled rooms whose windows the guardian, who goes ahead of us, opens one after another endlessly—so noisily! and there are shutters in front of the panes, the light darts like a glance into the dusky rooms—figures, Leda, the Virgin, stir for a second in the dream, figures whose sky-blue August colours time has drowned, a sky riddled with a thousand swallow cries, under the shimmery water of brown varnish. Plunge, yes, plunge into the eddies and reflections of these layers of images, descend from level to level in the cool, fluid depths, now and then shot with sun, right to the bottom's push—and then rise again, O earth, transfigured, towards the pure sky, the leaves.

A NEW SERIES OF DISCOVERIES

August, now

I wrote that story, this was three months ago, and I sent it to Bruno Roy for his collection. I corrected the proofs, and some time after that I returned to Paris where I suddenly am curious about what exactly those 'Prague Discoveries' were, in their day. I trust my memory but it is based on such slender information! I'm surprised to be so ill-informed about what was really a rather extraordinary event, and what surprises me most of all—it's most unlike me—is that in all these years I've made no attempt to return to the sources. I had at least one article, from the *Burlington Magazine*—which, so far as I can recall, reached me two or three years after the discovery's first mention in the news; from time to time since then I would see myself opening the magazine on the day it arrived, noticing the article, scanning the first few lines. What's more, I had even been to Prague and visited the castle and its painting gallery at whose end on an appropriately sized wall, illuminated from the left, I would hazard—but why this particular memory?—I recognized an old friend, the Rubens, a huge, bizarrely magnificent canvas, a 'feast of the gods', with something picnicky about it, albeit frenzied and so very modern: hats à la Manet and laughter out of Offenbach. Having got that far I must have asked about a catalogue.

I scour my shelves for the catalogue but in the end I have to admit I don't have it.

Next I look for the article I recalled, and I do find one, in the right magazine and from more or less the period I had in mind—'Rediscovery of Old Masters at Prague Castle', by T. Gottheiner, in 1965; it must be translated from German—but this time I cannot not notice the absence of any reference to the lost room of the original newspaper article. Indeed, this account, apparently well informed, and cautious, God knows, implicitly denies its existence, in that the room does not figure in the detailed description of the discovery. Didn't I read Gottheiner's article when I first saw it? I could, in the ensuing years, have sworn I had, even if I ended up thinking, contradictorily, I grant you, that I still had to inform myself more precisely about the finding of the forgotten place, the crossing of its threshold, the discovery of the paintings. And my belief that I'd read it was all the more compelling as, ever since the *Burlington* article, I'd kept in mind both an idea of the Rubens and the names of a few painters, Italians mostly, Mannerists or 'Seicento-esques', whose works they'd found.

At this point I call one of my friends who I know will have a copy of the Prague catalogue. He reads me a few excerpts —no, nothing. Everything happened just as T. Gottheiner describes and it is true that not much gets hushed up—what could they fear?—in the reports of peaceful historians. In a nutshell, the paintings from the imperial collections, once kept in the castle, stolen during periods of pillage, or sold, or moved elsewhere—all this remains vague—had not all reappeared, far from it, in the museums of the rest of the world or in art sales; and after the last war, when they undertook a complete inventory of the Hradčany, they were at first amazed by what was missing; then they told themselves that in that huge, long-ruined building there were a number of canvases whose paint was flaking off or drowned under successive coats of varnish, canvases no longer looked at when people went by them—rarely—in the dim rooms; and they began to restore and study them. It now appeared that works they'd decided were mediocre, of no great interest, by followers —decided when, in fact, and where? nowhere, never, it's just that time had gone by without anyone noticing—were in many instances the beautiful paintings they'd been seeking in vain in the four corners of the earth. A 'return of the hidden', but with nothing very remarkable about it. Gottheiner's story is only slightly complicated—but no, it is I really, even today unable to make myself read everything—by allusions to a 'Guardian of the Treasure', said to have occupied, at certain periods, a *Kunstkammer*, a room of artworks, where several of the lost painting may have hung right up to the recent inspections. Might we have there in this first museum the origin of the information, definitely erroneous, by which I was so complacently taken in? A place they talked of in the castle, a place they'd heard of but whose location in the labyrinth of rooms they no longer knew? Nothing in any case that would have comforted me in my myth of the long walled-up door if, during my visit to the Hradčany, I'd glanced at the catalogue as I nearly always feel compelled to do.

What to conclude? I've been thinking about this new series of discoveries, which, needless to say, troubles me considerably, and I believe there are two possible hypotheses.

The first, easy hypothesis is that until I could, for whatever reason, write down the first pages of my story, I unconsciously protected the initial scrap of information, the one that set me daydreaming, from all other evidence. I wanted to safeguard, let's say, this flash of thought from below so long as favourable 'circumstances'—never mind which—hadn't allowed it to catch fire all of a sudden in some detour of my writing.

But I also wonder—what am I saying, this is the greater temptation, it's already a sort of certitude—whether my emotion or fascination or fear—this feeling, it is difficult to express in one word in French; the *Burlington Magazine*'s word, unusual for them, was *awe*:[13] magnificent, the fear exceeding a visible cause—hadn't, on the contrary, found in Gottheiner's article not the denial that needed to be pushed aside so the reverie could continue but a confirmation, even one so disquieting, in its unexpected additional information that as soon as I had read the text—yes, well and truly read it—I had to promptly repress the dangerous revelation.

What does he say, in effect, Gottheiner—a name I keep writing Gottenheir; my pen has got mixed up several times, I must be hearing 'the inheritor' (*the heir* in English) of the gods (*Götter*, in German), but why the devil? If not that in a kind of half-light, a silence, some paintings they believed lost, paintings they thought were *elsewhere* were in fact *here*? Absent they were present. Or again, what was offered to their attention—those vague works on the walls, like this or that speech act, with a meaning but also a reason to pronounce it, the beginnings of an interpretation, a glimmer of law at least in the disorder of the signs—was *other*, and would one day be recognized as such, with eyes suddenly other? An evidence? But no, a lure! An image, no, the sheet of water that gleams in peace, one might say, but which hides a whole life, of which the marshy mass of brown varnish should have given them a premonition all the same. And this is indeed a terrifying piece of news, for Prague Castle is not the only Prague Castle. The lost gallery, the unknown we don't want—I am discovering that these things are in each of our words, our desires, and trouble with their shimmering or their mirages our consciousness that fancies itself free.

So I hypothesize that if the first news item I came across about the walled rooms and the works hidden from view, refused to our knowledge, struck me by its symbolic possibilities, in which the unconscious signifies—the unconscious being the locus of our images and our forbidden and perhaps impenetrable fears—the second article, considerably more suggestive and pressing—truer, simply—reminded me that the murky depths are never so distant that we can hide them from ourselves for long, and that we will be able to conjure them up again even if this entails some fear. The first piece of news was, all told, reassuring; it said consciousness is a 'castle' without secret regions aside from those that are closed or which, if need be, can be again closed; and very little had to be added to this piece of news to preserve its unexpected promise, nothing but a sort of myth—of a cave-in, a closing-off—that one would guard preciously in one's memory, along writing's perilous roads. The other piece of news, on the contrary, is what we don't want to know, since we have to go on living.

Can we allow ourselves to think—engaged as we are in an existence, with its necessary train of beliefs, with its attachments, with the desire for meaning that emerges as soon as a destiny takes shape—that all these values, these colours, even these presences we assemble, are less our true knowledge, our freely assumed responsibility, than a simple aggregate of words endlessly uttered in the place of others, and riddled with errant forces, impulses that in their emptiness know nothing of what we believe we want? Should we become aware of this eternal doubling of any act and all things, right away what solitude, for, no, it's not that the disavowed 'I' ceases to be, it goes on thinking within us, it feels, it still desires, but henceforth it has nothing—this earth is an exile, even 'dotted with flowers' like the loveliest painting. Ah, better to repress instantly the most dangerous part of the revelation! And what better way to accomplish this than by recounting it, but changed—confronting it while displacing its too-threatening signs? Thus one writes books . . .

February

Yes—I pick up these last few pages again, I reread them, rediscover them rather—yes, one can say what they say, these thoughts make sense. How to live if one is not the origin? If at least one does not reflect the distant being, the indifferent being, in the mirageless depths of a bright mirror?

But if this is so then why did I let myself understand, last summer, what I would previously have rejected—the paintings' true location, which the text composed in May seems unaware of, in the old Hradčany? Why this need for more information scarcely three months later? Isn't this new desire the real enigma?

Back I go again to 'The Prague Discoveries', which I am still not able to consider done. One astonishing thing, all the same, dating from their very first period—that I then, abruptly and, what's more, without encountering any obstacles, undertook to draft this story, or story about the idea of a story, that I'd kept to myself for twenty-odd years (a long time) without ever very seriously thinking about writing it down. Was there some event at about this time or slightly earlier that triggered this decision?

I reread, it's still difficult, the sentences printed and published. I make myself look from the outside at each of these words I chose.

And I notice first that they do indeed lend themselves to the myth of the sealed door. In these very same words, though, in which the unknown is once more sealed off, in which the phantasmic stones roll endlessly into the depths, a concern, a memory, an anguish, keeps rising to the surface; and, alongside the perturbed 'historian', another person, alert and questioning, keeps watch; someone who whole-heartedly refuses the distance that is being recreated, the silence that seals up. In other words, my story cannot be reduced to the two dimensions and linear unity of the mythic discourse. Granted, it's not the novel I regretted the second day; still, it evokes people and places and even feelings that seem to exceed with their existential, irrational and ambiguous thickness my attempts at a plot. It may be that my disquiet worked from the start as a kind of censorship, in itself like a dream. I must however acknowledge in its work the desire for something more, and all this creates a sort of dream within a dream, a dream whose dispersed elements are not, even so, without coherence nor perhaps their own particular truth.

So all that remains for me to do now is reassemble, so as to recommence understanding them, the details that proliferated, in sum, where being was suddenly absent—perhaps, as if in response. Why this young woman who 'swims through her days', why this house in the mountains—where again there are paintings—why, further, this bed 'on which they have both lain down, she no longer sees his face', why did I complicate the historian's 'metaphysical' confession with the hint of a carnal union? And why this open window—a question I ask myself in the text itself—why the vast calm outside which at the end replaces the man, the woman, the drama of the one and the other, and foregrounds 'all those stars wrapped in the haze of the Milky Way—and something like a form breathing in this mist'?

'Something . . .' I attest I wrote the sentences I've just quoted just as I imagined the story they belong to—compelled, ignorant, that is, of what I was saying in them, and with no intention of signifying something either through allusion or symbol. That's how it was, and even if I saw clearly that my reverie, as I said, forms an indecomposable whole, I could not have explained what the shape in the mist signified or represented. Insofar as it was unfinished or lacking, I might perhaps have concluded 'God', without forgetting however that such an interpretation would have contravened the suggestion of a futurity whitening in the image. Deeply rooted within me, in effect, is the sense that what we name Faith is impossible.

God! And yet there is a God, in the preceding pages, at the ambiguous level where many words in the lexicon of historians keep us, especially when the topic is Italian painting. I note: *Visitation* and *Magi*. And I can't dissimulate from myself that as soon as *Annunciation* is mentioned very little 'scientific' neutrality remains, since the Annunciation is the subject of the work that so perturbs my hero, as his words show. The Angel, the Virgin. And 'it's the vase too, it's the flower.' The mother who is sometimes shown on a meadow 'dotted with flowers'—rarely in Florence or Rome, granted, but in Germany and Bohemia . . . From one theme to the next in any case, always a divine birth.

So all I have left to do today is to understand at last what I've known for a long time, needless to say, since 'it was written' so precisely: that is, this 'something like a form', but which breathes; this presence, as yet uncertain but obviously desired, is a coming birth, a birth as vast as the starry sky, the earth, a birth that might be divine—save that any birth is divine, all life taking shape is a new earth and a new sky, whence it follows that the desire expressed in my story, helped by the bed, the nearness of two beings, the aromatic mountain's surrounding silence, does not perhaps call for much theology. God, no, the child as manifestation in itself, the only true one, the only evident one, of what always seeks and loses itself in the idea of God, naive, in sum.

I knew this; even my conscious thought knew it to some extent, my 'philosophy' that floods in so easily now, a timeless intuition, to back up my reading! For I am not unaware (what am I saying, I have repeated, harped on, used it as the epigraph to at least two books) that the experience of nothingness, as I have said, the feeling of exile in the very spot in which one has one's being, and of the self as a sort of image, is merely what one feels when one is wrapped up in oneself, without any real outside responsibility, with the result that one cannot write, or act, except starting from one's own obsessive life: whereas a decentring occurs immediately, effacing doubt and its mirages, if another life appears beside our own, a still-fragile presence that will need to be helped to its unknown maturation. Who can think for long that he is not, if it is granted him to make being? Whether one believes oneself nothing or not, one no longer has time to spend brooding, and not only in ordinary duration but also on the level of reflection where doubt, that distraction, ceases to be an option. One is the son of one's child, that's the whole mystery. And what fades, in these moments, as the story already indicated with its obsessive use of a few words—other, different, unknown—is not just one's anguish about the ultimate being of the 'me', but also one mode of being of the 'me'. 'Before', at the stage of the 'historian', let's say, pretty much all one knew of oneself was the enigma of one's particularity: the feeling that one is a product of chance, a fluke—deprived of being and active nonetheless, exigent, eternal naysayer in one's absurd writing—that at times haunts us like a double, all the more strange and pernicious as it has our traits, almost our way of looking at things. I don't doubt any longer, now. The 'Prague Discoveries' were only for the sake of dreaming that the 'bad' unknown, a mirage born of the vertigo, be replaced by this other, saving, unknown: one's ignorance of the future, the ordinary day-to-day future, in a life that gives us jobs to do.

If I was able at last to write this text after having kept it for such a long time on this side of the words like a dream afraid to avow itself, it's because at the end of this waiting period, the 'something like a form' breathed in a real mist, moved—after which a birth occurred. Now I could let the old desire be expressed, I could even signify it accomplished, for what does it seek to say after all, this new 'idea' I had, that came along to re-colour the first idea—the idea that the underground room, archaic den for the double, also receives the light through an opening it has, who knows how? The nocturnal window of the room in the mountains has now become a bay shot through with sun. And the enigma's jux-taposing of two visions, two relationships to the eternal light, indicates not just that an event has occurred, in a life; it is a sort of graft whence a new kind of utterance that aspires to be time's daughter, touches, through the writing, the obscure rootstock of dreams.

RUE TRAVERSIÈRE

When I was a child I fretted a good deal about a certain cross-street whose name was Cross Street—Rue Traversière, rather. At one end, not too far from our house and the school, it was the everyday world while at the other end, over there . . . Meanwhile the flashing lights of the street's name promised that it truly was the passage.

And I kept my eyes open whenever we walked down it, as occasionally happened, and we even went right to the far end of it, as if it were the same as any other street, but when I reached the far end I was tired, nodding off, and all of a sudden there was the bizarre space of the big botanical garden. —'Is it here,' I would ask myself, 'that over there begins? Here, at this house with its drawn shutters? Here, under this lilac? And this group of children playing with their hoops, and their marbles, on this pavement with weeds pushing up through the cracks, isn't one of them already on the far side, isn't he touching the hands of the little girls from over there with his shadowy fingers?' Notions of course contradictory, fleeting. All the more so as these modest houses, their vaulted backyards, in no way set themselves off from many others in our city; one sensed, one breathed right to the last painted metal door only the excess torpor of the suburbs and their kitchen gardens. How bland the face of what really matters! When we reached the botanical garden with its odour of otherness, where each tree wore a name tag, I raced off, jolted awake; I wanted to go far, enter elsewhere, but the paths must have turned in the shade of the boxwood and looped back to where they began, for I soon found myself yet again at the point of departure.

How good it was for me this name of Rue Traversière; and this garden of plant collections; and the vegetable Latin of the early evenings with their damp heat!

Five years ago when my mother was in the hospital beside the botanical garden, I returned to the Rue Traversière two or three times in the early afternoon. All at once, after so many years away, I rediscovered the almost forgotten childhood city and this street which seemed to open onto another world.

Still the same prudence—or even peace; still the smell of wet lettuce in front of the doors, the old women in the windows, eternally stitching at faded linens, the same Byzantine peacocks face to face in the lace of the dining-room curtains, one fluttering, perhaps, for a moment. And the chalky tuff still crumbling at the corners of walls. And the children, silent. No, Rue Traversière hadn't changed. And yet . . .

How to say this? It seemed to me that here, where I was, and there, where I was going, all together were what at one time I could only locate on the margins, in the invisible.

RETURN, IN THE EVENING

An alley in the botanical garden, with a good deal of red sky above damp trees. And a father and a mother from the steelworks who have brought their child here.

Then, on the evening side, the roofs are a hand that offers a stone to another hand.

And suddenly, it's a neighbourhood of shops, squat and dark, and the night which has been dogging our steps is panting, and sometimes the panting stops; and the mother is immense alongside the growing boy.

'Rue Traversière,' someone says to me in an art gallery one afternoon—standing in front of the window I can see grey walls, passers-by on the Rue Jacob—'Rue Traversière, oh, I recognized it in that piece you wrote, for—imagine—I too once lived in your city. How I loved its silence, and those big houses . . .'

'Big houses? No. It was a very poor street.'

'Not at all! I recall every detail. Gardens with walls, and trees. The archbishop's palace next door.'

'The archbishop's palace, no, absolutely not, it was the botanical garden.'

And so it goes; we evoke a part of town I, like him, know well, for I lived there as a teenager. Going to the *lycée* in those days I would sometimes cut through the archbishopric gardens, almost always deserted, coming out of them into empty streets. Shimmering, dangerous moments when I was tempted to shout, as loud as I could, to prove to myself that I existed in my own way, to verify that these rows of private houses and gardens in which nothing stirred, not a sound, save for the eternal far-off piano on which a scale was being picked out—

to verify that this was, I would say, no, not even a décor, worse, the crystallization of an unknown matter, with stain-like windows devoid of meaning, doors deaf as the surrounding stone. Shout, do something, anything, to make a curtain twitch, the piano stop, then race off, book-bag thumping on your back, towards the little house of those days, near the canal, where my father had come to die. I know that neighbourhood well, and it's not Rue Traversière.

Unless . . . I've known with such utter certainty, and for so many years, that Rue Traversière runs west, into the outskirts, the first farms, into the dampness of lilacs and the wheezing of pumps. I even walked along it a few years ago when the city of my childhood reappeared, then faded again. Yet the thought that I'm mistaken has just entered and taken up residence in me.

I return to my present home and I look for the map I've kept of the city, a very old map that has been much consulted in the past, but carefully, a map showing signs of wear, taped together on the underside with strips of brown paper. It still unfolds, the words and the streets meet up, again the dead language speaks at the crossings. And it's true, Rue Traversière is in the east, in the rich part of town. And over here, running out into the shapeless suburbs, what is the name of that street I took again only six or seven years ago, mulling over its importance in my life?

I peer closer, eyes blurring, and find nothing. Still, here are several streets that run west, long, zigzagging a little, like former country roads city planners have haphazardly straightened, but it seems to me that I know each of them by heart, and none of them is the street I see so clearly when I close my eyes. And as for others, elsewhere, there are one or two whose strange names could have conjured up the idea of a 'cross street' and merged with it later—as for the Rue de la Fuye, which comes back out of the blue, it's really too far from the garden of animals and plants—this Botanical, in sum, was a little the Garden of Eden—Rue de la Fuye peters out in the south among the railway tracks. Where then is this street that I know with my whole being, which *is*, and what is it called? What is its real place in this network of places, equally real, which seem however to exclude it?

And asking myself these questions, here on the famous white page, repeating my astonishment to myself, nonetheless choosing my words, I know that this is still writing, I know that these new notations only continue *Rue Traversière,* the other account, and save a memory of being in nothing but error by complicating and giving weight to a poem. Still—

please believe me—the enigma that I am articulating is in my life too, the astonishment will endure longer than the words that express it. I can write and write, but I am also the person who looks at the map of the city of his childhood and doesn't understand.

Which was the *other* Rue Traversière? How could I have lived so long with two distinct kinds of knowledge, two memories that never crossed? Who is the person in me who begins when the other—or an other, and which other?—goes into the little house along the canal where there's a clump of bamboo in the pocket-handkerchief garden—where we came to live two years ago, where the father is dying, which we will soon leave?

I move these figures with their vague, worn outlines about my table—these faces, these lost gazes that redden, these memories of the corners of halls, the wallpapers' faded flowers, the door to the laundry room out back with its slippery step; smells, including the smell of the chestnut trees on the boulevard at each spring's bright mystery, of swallows skimming the ground when the stormy sky tilts, sweeping the past away, outlining—might that not be the future, over there, those men and women in the cloud, the laughter of colour over shining water, that body like froth in Polynesia.

Which card must I place on top of which other card; which one without faces, coloured crimson grey, unseeing, have I already laid over this other too-significant one, unless the latter has resurfaced from the shuffled deck like—irresistible, final—not the meaning's annulment but the meaning? I have many uncertain memories still to decipher, I see. A whole long Rue Traversière to move far away among my first chance happenings, my first darkly seen places, my troubled affections, right to the at once absolute and indifferent origin, the origin which, though poor, was nonetheless—creatures and plants, and the smell of boxwood, and the dim figures of the man and woman—a whole world that I owe to another child. Chance, of which we are born, chance precariously, delicately, endlessly folded over us like the chrysalis' wing; you can only keep all of it in the colours of your ignorance as long as we are alone and as if asleep, turned to the shadows. To the other —be it the writing, the wing's unfolding, every now and then—one owes the sense.

A FIT OF LAUGHTER

It had something to do with an old man whose speciality, and why not, was making wash drawings of laughter.

He is a sage, they said. For a long time all he has wanted to do is paint, with one broad sweep of his brush—yes, fits of laughter.

On tiptoe, through this covered passage at the back of the bamboo garden one approached the door to his cell. Listen, they whispered (someone was laughing, was laughing!), listen to the sound of the brush.

OF THE SIGNIFIER

The first word was 'the cloud', the second was again 'the cloud', the third, the fourth, etc., was 'the cloud' or 'the sky' or 'the air', or some such.

But the seventh, already, was getting torn, was fading, could no longer be differentiated from the tears, the erasure of others lower down, from others on and on endlessly, from others ash, from others almost a powder, white, that we would stir in vain in this large rough canvas bag, what was left of the language.

.

1 Cf. Stéphane Mallarmé's letter to Eugène Lefébure, '27 May 1867' in *Oeuvres Complètes* (Paris: Gallimard, 1998), p. 721 (YB, conversation, September 2013).

2 Piero della Francesca.

3 Cf. Arthur Rimbaud, 'Vagabonds' (*Les Illuminations,* 1873–75): '. . . moi presséd de trouver le lieu et la formule' (I in a rush to find the place and the formula) (YB, conversation, November 2013).

4 The master referred to is Mallarmé (YB, conversation, November 2013).

5 Cf. Charles Baudelaire, Sonnet XCIII: 'À Une Passante' (To a Passer-by): 'crispé comme un extravagant' (rigid as an extravagant).

6 Piero della Francesca painted *The Madonna del Parto* around 1460 for the church of Santa Maria de Momentana. It was moved, following an earthquake in 1785, to the chapel in the Monterchi village cemetery. Since 1992 it has been in the Museo della Madonna del Parto in Monterchi.

7 This was a kind of candle, made by enrobing a long hemp wick in wax, that one slipped one's arm into like a bracelet, to visit the catacombs (YB, conversation, November 2013).

8 'Rome, the Arrows.'

9 Piero della Francesca's paintings *The Flagellation of Christ* and *The Madonna of Senigallia* were stolen from the Ducal Palace in Urbino in 1975 and only recovered a year later.

10 Presence: 'to feel a thing or a being in the immediacy and the fullness of what they are in themselves, rather than seeing in them only the for ever abstract idea we have of them owing to language's categories and prejudices [. . .].' Yves Bonnefoy, 'Grec et en français' in *L'autre langue à portée de voix: essais sur la traduction de la poésie* (Paris: Seuil, 2013), pp. 133–42; here p. 135.

11 *Rue Traversière* was first published in 1977.

12 Cf. Mallarmé: '*Salut*' (Cheers): 'Nothing, froth, virgin verse . . .'.

13 In English in the original.